Secrets
of a Successful Relationship
Revealed

Secrets of a Successful Relationship Revealed

Find Passionate and Juicy
Peace and Joy
— not Conflict and Anger

By Phil and Maude Mayes

Olive Branch Communications, Inc.
Santa Barbara, California, 2011

Book design by Phil and Maude Mayes
Cover design by Phil Mayes
Photography by Phil Mayes
100% Factor photographer Kathee Miller featuring
Nebula Dance Lab

ISBN 978-1466451735

Printed in the United States of America

For Annie and Sam Amato,
for teaching love and living love.

Table of Contents

Acknowledgments

We would like to thank Jennifer Phelps and Richard Niles for their close and personal reading and editing of the manuscript. We are especially indebted to C. Barrie Bedell for his insistence on printing a book as well as an ebook, and for his invaluable advice on its presentation. Thanks to Jean Kaplan, whose sharp eyes found several major typos, even after the book was edited. We appreciate the advice of Temogen Amato and Jinjee Talifero, who helped us into the modern age of social networking. Finally, we are grateful to our numerous friends for taking their valuable time to read and share their responses to the book.

Introduction

❝ Do you realize that in the year that we've known each other, we've never argued?"

We were in a log cabin in Central California, celebrating our first anniversary of meeting, and it was just starting to become clear to us that our relationship was out of the ordinary. In the years since then, we have been astounded again and again by the peaceful nature of our union. We live with an amazing lack of conflict and an ever increasing experience of joy, ease and harmony. In fact, this experience is so profound, that we both feel compelled to share it with others.

Our goal is not a small one. We wish to be a part of spreading peace on Earth between people. We are convinced that some of the things we have learned from our time together can be applied to any and all relationships, romantic or not. It's not our intention to offer rules for how relationships should be, for every one is different. Instead, we have chosen to share how we are, with the idea that when something resonates, you will be able to apply it in your own way, and by doing so, bring more peace and harmony into your life.

After some years of experiencing our unusually successful union, we started to explore it in writing together. We chose the forum of a blog, and for several years wrote back and forth to each other. At a certain point, we reviewed all the blogs, and a number of themes emerged, which we have put together in this book. We wrote the introduction to each theme and then selected blog entries to illustrate and expand on them. The themes are tightly interwoven, so the writings in each chapter echo and connect to the others.

These ideas are simple but very powerful. We believe that if you are open to the possibility of a different way of relating, of changing your frame of reference, a magical transformation can take place. We know from our experience that it is real and tangible: not a theory, not thoughts, not a collection of ideas. We hope you can find inspiration for your own life in what we have shared.

" Once the realization is accepted that even between the closest human beings infinite distances continue, a wonderful living side by side can grow, if they succeed in loving the distance between them which makes it possible for each to see the other whole against the sky."

RAINER MARIA RILKE

Individuality

One of the key characteristics of our relationship is a deep respect for the separate individuality of the other person. We both have a very strong sense of our identities. Neither of us would be comfortable letting go of or changing our inner person. We would not respond favorably to being told how to act or how to be. As a result, we do not try in any manner to alter, re-form or impinge upon the other. We do not push, pull or adjust who the other is or should be. And yet, we have opened ourselves up to a deep merging union with each other.

Furthermore, we take pleasure in seeing such autonomy in action. We honor and celebrate the difference. We feel enriched by another person who is actually different; has a different thought pattern, history and a different way of expressing things.

To grant such autonomy to the other needs trust. This is something that was assumed in the beginning, then confirmed over a period of time. This confirmation is found not in small things like remembering to pick up milk, but through a consonance of meanings and values: how do we see other people, and how do we treat them? Once these values are seen to be aligned, differences are not threatening or disturbing, and we can relax and revel in the uniqueness of the other.

We have shared our deepest inner places and have at the same time retained two totally independent and separate lives. As these mesh more and more, we continue to be present as two whole individuals, even as we deepen in our union.

Maude: Other Personalities

Dear Phil,

It occurs to me that we have some basic behaviors that figure in an important way in our relating.

We seem to both have a great respect for the sacrosanct nature of each and every personality. We are not trying to change each other, we are not judging each other, we are not trying to tell each other what to do or how to behave. In fact, that is so far from how we are with each other, so foreign to how we are with each other, that I must conclude that this is integral to our loving and conflict free relationship. We do not do this with others either.

Phil: Why Does it Work?

We do something, and it just works, and this happens time and time again. Yes, I know there are many areas where we're a fit on paper: same age, politics, etc., but there are some areas that appear mismatched: different culture, different childhoods, you raised children and I didn't. Yet we have this way of agreeing on things and flowing through life that is uncanny in its easiness, or to put it another way, I hardly ever feel that I have compromised at all. Instead, we each suggest possibilities until we reach something that satisfies both of us. My self, my integrity, remains intact.

Maude: Union with Two Separate
Personalities Remaining Intact

I want to comment on your remark that "I hardly ever feel that I have compromised at all. My self, my integrity, remains intact". I agree. Although there is nothing wrong with compromise, it doesn't describe what we do. I don't feel like either of us gives anything up. In fact, we seem rather to gain something. We don't impinge on the nature of each of our separate and distinct personalities. We experience union, and yet remain totally ourselves, totally whole, with no part of that distinct individuality being altered, or crowded out or in any way threatened. In fact, it seems we celebrate the uniqueness that is each of us, while finding so much common ground.

Phil: Talking

My Dear Maude,

I am blown away by how we are. I have never experienced this harmony of being with anyone else. The way we flow through the world together, taking things just as they come, is like nothing I have ever experienced. With others, there were always periods of conflict, friction, disagreements. With you, I have, for the first time, the experience of always being on the same side. If we want different things, we talk – just talk! – until the choice becomes clear.

I can say whatever comes to mind, and you just hear me. That is SO liberating. And every time it happens, it makes it easier to speak truth the next time.

Maude: I'm Me and You're You

I'd like to try to break down some of the qualities that seem so important to how we are with each other.

One factor that seems critical is not only accepting the other person for who they are, but also celebrating with joy who they are, feeling a deep abiding affection and respect for the other.

At the same time, it is important not to get confused and think that one's identity has merged with the other. We seem to keep our separate identities, while merging into something else as well. When you're not trying to change the other person, you don't run into so many of the difficulties that bring conflict and distance between two people. So how does one find a balance of not trying to change each other, while at the same time being open to help and support each other?

I think part of this paradox could be avoided by not thinking you know better than your partner what is right or best for them. Maybe by not separating yourself from your partner, by not thinking from a position of separation such as smarter or better or more fully knowing what right action is, you can instead actually experience the joy of another viewpoint, the discovery of other ways to see and think of things. This difference of identity has to at the same time be consonant with your basic values. You have to feel connected and in accord, to fully appreciate difference and not want to make it the same as you.

Phil: Staying Connected

We always feel connected. When you leave physically, I don't feel that anything has changed between you and me, and when we come together again, there is no need for any adjustment. This happens after sex, too; there is no break in intimacy. All this contrasts with former relationships, which interleaved connection and alienation.

So what are we doing differently?

I think with others, I withdrew to regain my sense of self, because I had lost it in several ways. One was the limitations on behavior that many people impose. Another was the need for silence; as an introvert (and I was more so in those days), too much company too long was exhausting. Lastly, the experience of merging with another, though ecstatic, was a different unfamiliar world, and maybe after a while I had to return to the familiar.

To stray from the personal a bit, I think many people connect from a sense of incompleteness; they want the other to assuage their needs, substitute for their inadequacies, fix their sense of loss, grief, pain. This only works for a while, as the underlying needs reappear; they must be confronted on their own, not salved by taking from another. For the partner, the constant supply of support can become a Sisyphean task.

With you, none of these happen. I do not have to watch myself when I am with you, because you let me be who I am. Oh, thank you! I cannot say it enough. You have your own need for space and silence, as do I, and because we remain connected, it is effortless to separate, and to rejoin later. And lastly, I welcome the ecstasy, and experience it as an addition to myself, not as an alternative. `

So to summarize, we remain connected, yet I always feel completely myself. It is paradoxical, yet indisputable.

Maude: Identity Confusion

We do not confuse our identities, which I believe happens in a lot of relationships. I do not feel that you are actually me, and that therefore you should do everything as I would do it and act as I would. I am not censoring or judging or changing or improving upon who you are. You do none of this with me either. And yet, we are very supportive of each other, always wanting the very best for the other in every way.

Phil: Work and Space

My Dear Maude,

I have been deeply involved in work for the last few days. In the past, that has been very threatening to my partners; they interfered, pouted, accused me of withdrawal, demanded more of me.

With you, no. You give me the space to be myself, do what I want to do, just as you always do. Thank you, thank you, thank you. The shadow of the past still makes me cautious, makes me check to see how you are, but hallelujah, everything is fine. That is why I say thank you.

Maude: Being with You as You Are and Celebrating That

We don't seem to be busy with or involved in wanting our partner to be anything other than who and what they are.

If you can actually be with another person, without wanting them to change, or being busy in any way to alter them, then amazing things become possible.

For this magic to work, you have to actually be suited to the other. There has to be a match, a balance of energy between you. At the same time, there is a joy of being with someone who is innately different than you — someone who is not you, but another.

I love experiencing who you are and how you interact with the world. I so enjoy the way you take pleasure in who I am, and I do have the feeling you truly see me for who I am.

Phil: Being Suited

I agree about needing to be suited to the other. I don't want to make a list of areas, as it's probably different for everyone. But once those are met, that's the time to leave well enough alone, to let the other person be who they are, and we do that so well! I am amazed again and again at how we do that.

Recognizing this suitability and giving it priority is a difficult thing to do early in life because there is also sexual attraction that is so powerful, yet seems completely independent of other elements. I have seen people drawn again and again to a completely unsuitable relationship, though in several cases I'm thinking of, I can't say how much it was sex and how much it was a working through of some childhood relationship.

So yes, we're very suited, though I haven't got a list in my head of what those reasons might be. Like many things between us, I seem to have made decisions at some subconscious level. In fact, both of us seem able to trust our subconscious/intuition/whatever name you wish to use. This intuitive element is very important, and maybe other people ignore it and instead focus on things like similar interests. They're important, though it doesn't have to be a complete match, but interests alone don't cut it. There has to be some – gee, I'm inclined to get cosmic here and say energy or harmony or something that describes a resonance of some sort between people. And there also needs to be a similarity of world view – people, politics, religion – or at least, no radical differences.

Maude: Imagine Treating the Other Exactly as You Treat Yourself

So many of my friends who are not in a partnership tell me that they are very happy with their lives. They feel that their lives are rich and full. Even so, they would like a partnership in their life. At the same time they imagine that they would have to give up some of what they like about their lives, give up freedom of choice and space, if they were to let another into their intimate space.

If they honor the other person the same way they do themselves, if they don't try to alter or make the other different, then maybe the other won't do it to them either. Maybe one could start out not giving up freedom or space, but just adding to life what feels good and what you want to do or share with the other person. Maybe as a starting image you can use addition and not giving up. If you honor the other and see them as a complete and total individual just like you, then instead of personal encroachment there will be enrichment for each.

❝ Love is union with somebody, or something, outside oneself, under the condition of retaining the separateness and integrity of one's own self."

ERICH FROMM

Our Process

I t's hard to pinpoint when it began, but a definite process has developed whereby we solve problems, make decisions and come to courses of action. Whether we are dealing with something large or small, we seem to follow a similar path.

Something is put forth for consideration. Each of us speaks our minds to the issue. We both listen fully to the ideas and thoughts of the other. There is no feeling of tension. Neither of us is steering the exchange to a particular conclusion. The atmosphere is without charge, and there is no one pushing to be right.

As we continue to share and hear each other, a new element begins to arise that is not the original thought or idea from either of us. It is usually something better than what we individually brought to the topic. We have come together and co-created something new, yet neither of us has compromised. There have been no trade-offs nor any sense of winning or losing. The answer has grown out of the way we are together. It has come forth because we are wholly open and undefended in our sharing with each other.

In any situation there are many choices and outcomes. Often people lock onto a view and cannot let go of it to allow another one in. Our response to each other's input is almost exactly the opposite. We eagerly hear the ideas and thoughts of the other. We have no desire to coerce the other; there is no joy in a course of action that is not mutual.

The more we do this, the better we get at it, because we have the accumulated experience of how good the results are each time. This process brings a delightful sense of peace and pleasure with it. It is such a good feeling to experience the answers and solutions that emerge. They are always so much more than either of us had separately.

Maude: Being Right

One of the things that I love about how we are together is the lack of either one of us 'needing to be right' or being concerned with 'who is right'. When we listen to each other as we are talking together, we are actually listening. We are not just in our head, waiting for the moment when we can talk again about why our opinion is the correct one. In fact, both of us seem to really get off on the fact that the other one has different ideas and doesn't see everything exactly as we do. These differences are not really sources for actual conflict. They are not differences in meanings and values. I feel that in so many relationships, the sharing is more like a debate or an argument. Things that are often of no consequence or actual substance, become the areas of intense struggle, all in the name of 'who is right'!

By eliminating this type of back and forth altogether, we seem to wind up in a miraculous space. We go to an area where we share what each of us feels and thinks and even as we are talking, something begins to occur. We start to hear new ideas, things that aren't exactly from either of us, but yet have the best of what each of us has contributed. By the time we are done, we usually have a new creation, an answer to our problem or a plan for action that is much better than anything either of us came up with. It really feels like magic and it happens every time.

Phil: How We Agree

Dear Maude,

I have been mystified how we reach agreement on things. For instance, I wrote "We come to agreement on what we do together without apparent effort or decision-making" and "This happens so regularly that it is a statistical impossibility that we should always want the same things."

The other night you answered this so eloquently; let me see if I can summarize it.

It's a result of being open and present. You have an idea of what to do. I suggest something else that is not in your mind. Because you are open and undefended you are not stuck on your idea being the best. More than that, you welcome the variety and difference that another person brings to the table. Maybe it's not to your liking, but that's OK, too, because I am not bound to my suggestion. And so it goes, and we rapidly reach a conclusion that works for both of us. This whole process takes place so easily and fluidly that I think we must sometimes not see it happening, only experience the results.

It's aided by several things. That we like many of the same things broadens the area for agreement, but more than that is being open to newness and change, and not being attached to specific outcomes. Lastly, we have no desire to triumph over the other, and want what is best for both of us. This all takes a certain level of self-knowledge and non-attachment.

Maude: What is Important to Us?

I'm still very wrapped up in that conversation we had over the weekend.

We were talking about what normally causes discord and disharmony between couples. At the same time, we looked at what we do instead, as neither of us is attracted to either of those.

The specifics are rarely important to us. Therefore, neither of us is attached to specific outcomes. We do seem to have a lovely flowing dance by which we come to decisions, make plans and act together. Lack of attachment seems to be part of the entrance ticket to this altered state of union we experience: lack of attachment to the specifics, to being right, or to having the present altered by a predetermined image.

What is clearly very important to us is meaning and value, truth, beauty, goodness and love. As we are in harmony in these areas, we find our way through all the specifics without attachment, with joy and lightness!

Phil: Balance without Compromise

My Dear Maude,

Last night we came together late and just hung out, did the crossword, talked. We both said how delightfully cozy it was, and so the question arises again, how do we do this? The scientist would say that we each adjust our expectations and behavior to synchronize with the other, but look as I may, that is not what I see, for if that were the case, I would expect to see compromise, trade-offs, weighing the pros and cons. I don't. Instead, I see a process that is non-verbal, that I don't "make decisions", but instead, the activities "come to me". But it does feel intentional on another level. It feels as though we eschew words and thoughts and planning and allow some natural balance to take place. It is like trusting the us and not letting "words with charge", to use your memorable phrase, take over.

The result is a feeling of incredible lightness, airiness, freedom, liberty.

Many years ago I had the opportunity to ride rear-seat on a tandem. I was used to steering on a bike, and I jerked the handlebars so fiercely that the forward rider could not keep the machine in balance. Neither of us is doing that now.

Maude: Last Night is a Good Example

Last night is a good example of our process. We were discussing what we had in mind for our evening. You wanted to be sexually playful. I was favoring some hanging out and maybe some movie shorts. We talked and shared and then wound up doing something else. Something that wasn't what either of us had mentioned as possibilities, but came up from both of us being together and was completely unexpected and different and delicious.

We allow something new and unexpected to happen by not freeze framing a specific outcome or activity. This seems to be a key to our creativity together. We appear to co-create our experiences through some process where we sync in with each other and then just let it happen.

Phil: Equality

My Dear Maude,

We don't argue. Realization of that was the genesis of our exploration of our relationship. We've said "Oh, we don't argue because we don't want to", and that is part of it, but in addition to that, we are able to come to a mutually agreeable decision every time.

Now that is no doubt made simpler by our having similar opinions on tidiness, money, work, politics and more (though anyone who picks a seriously mismatched partner is either inexperienced, masochistic, or working through issues), but it's not that we always come from the same place initially. After listening to you, I find within myself something else that would work for me just as well; I can do this because I don't feel the need to hold to a particular opinion. You do likewise, and so we continue to listen to each other and look for something that works for both of us.

Another thing is (to steal your term) the celebration of difference – that the other introduces a variety into life that would not otherwise be there, and we welcome change rather than fearing it. Doing so is easier because of our mutual benevolence – that we don't want to take any course of action that will harm the other, so in the light of that, it is easy to trust the choices and suggestions of the other.

Maude: We Always Talk

As we were having our walk around the park this morning, you began a discussion of how we are doing on the bigger issues of our life together.

It was so good to just walk and talk. We always talk about things. I think this is a very important part of our process. We have a gentle way of sharing verbally and it keeps us in touch with each other and our feelings in a special way. We are always connected even when apart. However, communicating about everything on a constant

and regular basis gives us a very present moment know-
ledge of how the other is perceiving things.

I feel so much richer hearing our life through your
words and always hearing how you feel. It is so great that
we can speak and always feel heard, that we communicate
without judgment or special agendas. We always want the
best for each other and seem to feel assured that the other
wishes the best for us!

Phil: Balance and Stillness

My Dear Maude,

I want to speak about balance. The way we act together
is very puzzling. We come to agreement on what we do
together without apparent effort or decision-making. Certainly there are times when only one of us feels tired,
talkative, sleepy, sexual, but mostly we concur on whether to
walk, what movie to watch, when to separate, and all those
other joint decisions. It's that process of deciding that is
obscure; there is no sense of pitting my needs against yours,
struggling until a winner emerges. There is scarcely ever
even a sense that we have different agendas at all. But how
can this be? We're different people with different clocks; the
odds of being in sync become more improbable the more it
happens.

It is as if we have moved our consciousness from our
individual selves to us, that incorporeal being that has both
our interests at heart. I don't invoke magical channels here;
it's likely that there are signals of body language, smell,

voice, etc. by which we adjust to each other. However, looking for the mechanism is really irrelevant, because the balance arises from our intentionality. We achieve this by being, not by doing, and the more still we are, the more intense the experience becomes.

Maude: We Can Shake It All Up and Let It Come Down Entirely Differently

Dear Phil,

We've been having those wonderful talks about how we are going to move forward in these next six months and in our life together. I so enjoy these creative jam sessions, especially because they are not just pipe dreaming. They often result in wonderful new paths and directions for us. There is something about the way we are able to speak the totality of our minds to each other, never in a defensive way, never withholding or protected. We both just put out the full thoughts we can come up with and somewhere in between, a new and wonderful different concept or plan emerges, one that is neither from you or me. It is the answer that arises through our process and it is a co-creation of our united being.

Maude: Our Willingness to Experiment

Dear Phil,

In looking at some of the things we've done together, our willingness to experiment has caught my attention. We seem to easily take on a project, a new way of being or doing for us. We decide (through our process) that we're going to do something new or different, and then we just move smoothly into it. There doesn't seem to be any resistance or reluctance to shift and change.

I think that this comes from being in presence. We don't hang on specifics, pre-images or concepts. We don't overhang our experiences with each other with preconceptions or projections of any kind. We seem to delight in discovering the other as an other. It's always new and always better.

I think this same state of presence enables us to take on new directions with ease.

I can't imagine where this wonderful journey with you will be heading, but I go there with joy!

Phil: Bedrock

My Dear Maude,

One of the main reasons for our lack of conflict is that we agree on the ground rules. The funny thing is that originally we were never explicit about them, with maybe the exception of sexual monogamy, and it wasn't until we came to write our wedding vows that we put our common understandings into words.

I love the way we did it. We sat side by side on the bed, and each wrote down what was important for us. Then we exchanged lists and talked about our responses to each item. Often, we had said the same thing in different ways.

We came back to this a number of times over several days, talking about everything until we had identified and clarified the essence of what we were saying, and out of this, we crafted our vows.

- I promise to be your partner and lover through life.
- I promise to dwell in love, to act from love, to hear with love, to speak from love.
- I promise to always be truthful and to share what I feel.
- I promise to recognize and honor who you are and to always remember that "you are you and I am me."
- I promise to choose the positive and strive toward the good and act in support of you always all ways.
- With these promises I celebrate our union and rejoice in the Grace that brought us together.

It was, as is always the case with you, a delightful organic process. There were no points of significant disagreement; maybe some of emphasis, at most.

I was about to say that because we have this shared agreement on how we live life together, there is no need for conflict, but that doesn't follow: we could still argue over which movie to see. That doesn't happen, because the choice of movie is just not that important. The sense of peace that comes from our joint understanding of how we live our lives together far outweighs my desire to see a particular movie!

Maude: Vows, Decision Making and Union

My Dearest Phil,
Thank you for your beautiful expression of how we

are! Yes, that says it exactly. In looking at our vows, I see that many of the things we have been talking about in these conversations are included in our vows. The respect for the other as an other, truthfulness, seeking for the positive, coming from love. These are true expressions of how we are with one another. Talking, truthfulness, ongoing honest communication...these are important underpinnings to everything. We seem to naturally stay in touch and share our thoughts.

Our decision making process has been so easy as a result. We just talk until we find some solution that pleases us both. Neither of us seems to want to push an opinion or a particular viewpoint on the other.

Even though this has come very naturally to us, I believe that this style is something that can be cultivated. I think couples can come from a place of trust and respect that will enable them to find solutions suited to the union, rather than only to the one or the other. While doing this, seek for the positive and come from love. It feels so much better than manipulation or force or pressuring or anger or self-righteousness or control or separation or aloneness. Go for the union!

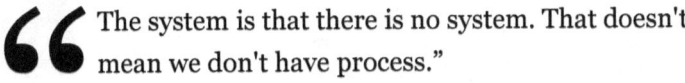 The system is that there is no system. That doesn't
mean we don't have process."

STEVE JOBS

The 100% Factor

In the beginning, like most new couples, we spent our time getting to know each other. We didn't do anything much out of the ordinary: beach walks, movie dates, dinners, drives in the country. We talked about everything, sharing our thoughts and ideals, and through this, learning each other's natures. Am I comfortable with this person? Are they trustworthy? At first, with little to go on, trust was an act of faith, a hope in the goodness of the other, but as we came to know each other through our words and deeds, that faith was justified. Our time together allowed us to see that our actions matched our words, and we came to recognize our shared meanings and values.

Here's where it gets a little tricky to describe. There was a point when we stopped all the measuring, the judging, the assessing, and accepted each other totally. From that point on, each of us could rest secure in the knowledge that our individuality, our unique personhood, would in no way be assailed by the other. We would not be questioned in our being; there would be no attacks, large or small, on our person; there would be no criticism, no demands, no attempts to change or control. We could each be ourselves completely without any fear of interference or pressure from the other.

This is what we refer to as the 100% factor: total acceptance of the other, of who and how they are. The extra-ordinary freedom to be yourself that comes from this kind of acceptance cannot be achieved by anything less than 100%. If there is some small corner within your partner that is still holding back acceptance, you never know when it might rear its head and bite you, so you must still always be guarded to some degree or another. But when each partner is assured of complete acceptance, it is transforming and wonderfully liberating; by being completely ourselves, we are that much more real, authentic and trustworthy to the other.

The effect of this complete openness cannot be emphas-ized enough. It produces a quantitative change in the experience. We have found that with this underpinning our relationship, there is no limit to the peace, love and joy that we can experience together. This openness feeds on itself, creating an ever-increasing bond. It fills us with strength and security to go about our daily challenges.

Maude: The 100% Factor

*We have coined a phrase recently that we call the 100%
factor that I think includes many of the aspects of our
togetherness.*

*The 100% factor refers to the element of being together
that enables total freedom from the need to withdraw and
to defend, and consequently to separate. The importance of
100% cannot be underestimated. 100% is nothing like 99%.
Anything less than 100% offers measurement, division, in
and out, good and bad.*

*I always love your example of a dance floor. If you
know that there is nothing on the dance floor, no
thumbtacks or other dangerous items, you can be free to
dance about, flying freely through the air, unmindful of
where you come down. As soon as you introduce one
thumbtack somewhere on the floor, you are no longer free
to leap and prance freely. You must always be careful you
don't come down on the tack and injure yourself. This very
knowledge inhibits you all the time, even if it's just a little
bit.*

*This is the same within relationships. The more
thumbtacks that appear in the exchange, the more you must
be careful, defended, withdrawn, on alert. Once you reach
the threshold of 100%, there is peace and joy and no
busyness in the mind about whether you are in or out, or
whether the person is right or wrong, or needs changing or
adjusting. You accept yourself and the other and go
forward in the freedom that this way of being brings.*

This is not a process. It is a transformation. You either

move into 100% or you don't. This way of being does not take work. In fact, it is quite effortless. You don't work on it, you just do it.

We have found that when we come together we are fully present, not experiencing the other through our pre-conceptions, rules and ideas, images of what should be or could be. We are there in comfort with ourselves and joyfulness in the other. We are not trying to make the other anything other than what they are, but rather rejoicing in what and who they are as it unfolds. There is a desire to share that which is; joy, beauty, goodness for example. There is no desire to make a point, to be 'right', to remake the other.

Phil: Behind the 100% factor

My dear Maude,

I want to make two points about the 100% factor — the principle of allowing each other total freedom, and how liberating that is.

The first is that I suspect people mishear it as 100% commitment. Yes, that's important too, but you can be 100% committed and a terrible nag. We are talking about something very different.

Secondly, we're not saying people should tolerate anything and everything, acting like a doormat and letting their partner walk all over them. Instead, it is only possible in a partnership that has core agreements in place. I think they vary from couple to couple, but examples would be trust, honesty, monogamy and fiscal responsibility. When these are in place, nothing else is necessary. You can give your partner the space to do and be anything.

Peculiarly, these agreements were never made explicit between us until we sat down to write our wedding vows. That must have been because our beliefs were communicated through our actions.

Maude: Empty-Mindedness Allows Something New to Happen

Since we spoke the other night, I have felt that it is really important for us to explore even further the quality of our path that you refer to as non-interference, and I usually refer to as relating to the other as a complete distinct personality. I believe that so much else of how we are, and the non-argumentative nature of our union, derives from this underpinning.

Is there a chicken and egg aspect here? We usually think that our strong presence with each other is brought about by this quality of non-interference. But I am beginning to wonder if it isn't a bit of both. Perhaps a kind of empty-mindedness is what enabled us to truly feel fully open enough to be together with this special kind of acceptance.

Lack of projections and demands is critical to being in this place together. Many people I know have their heads filled with everything they need to make things work, in any situation and in every relationship. They have so many things decided in advance – what they need in common and how things have to look and feel – that there is very little room for anything to actually just be, let alone the coming into being of something new.

I think that empty-mindedness, the willingness to let all ideas go and let new things happen, is a prerequisite to our path. The need for control and the sense of control have to be entirely abandoned.

Let's explore this as part of how we got here — to this wonderful place of peace and joy in love.

Phil: Emptiness

You ask about the origins of empty-mindedness. One was my experience of long, drawn-out arguments with shouting, crying, begging, withholding, accusing, sulking, withdrawing, and attacking. Words and acts from the past would be dragged in to make a case. Threats and demands would be made to gain the advantage. Finally, through exhaustion, we would reach a position where each of us would abandon the attack and just express our needs. It felt like a summer squall had blown in and passed over, leaving flooded paths, downed branches and litter all over. At that point we were able to hear the other person and accept their needs as real.

After a long time, I saw that the argument was merely the precursor to this place of communication and potential resolution. I never liked arguments, and these days, I choose to go directly to that post-squall place of self-expression without attack, that place where I can clearly distinguish between my own desires and my expectations of how other people should behave.

Maude: Yesterday Morning was Fun!

Dear Phil,

Yesterday we returned to our discussion of basic agreements which reframed itself into core values. This gives us a good place to find the 100% factor.

When you have core values as your basis for agreement and union, then you can let go of determining the specifics. You can celebrate that there is another person, one who is totally unique, and celebrate the difference. You can be constantly enriched by the other. We are able to reside in the present, experiencing what is, without pre-conceiving it. We don't try to fit the other into an idea or a mold or a picture of what should be or could be. We experience what is.

I think the sense of surety between us comes not only from our shared experiences, but also from these core values that we share about life and relationships.

Phil: Total Freedom

You talk about that wonderful metaphor of a thumbtack on the dance-floor, and how inhibiting even one can be. I want to expand on that a little. We've talked about this as 100% acceptance, and how different that is from 99%. It's not just

1% better; there is a qualitative difference to it. I can be myself without any little voice inside checking what I say and what I do. I can admire other women. I can say I want to work late. I can wear the same jeans all week. It's not that I am oblivious to your needs, for I enjoy doing things that bring you pleasure, but they never turn into expectations.

It is so liberating to have the space to be myself. In other relationships, after a while I found myself to be partially missing, as if small chips of myself had been destroyed over time, and I had to leave to experience my self again. I didn't see it in those terms so much at the time; it was more the experience of being in a cage and needing to roam free. I interpreted that (or my partners did for me) as a resistance to commitment, but now I am not so sure of that interpretation.

I don't have any of that with you. This is amazing to me, and I still cannot decide, after all this time together, how this has come to pass. I do know that an essential part of it is the total freedom that you grant me. Thank you, thank you, thank you.

" The intense happiness of our union is derived in a high degree from the perfect freedom with which we each follow and declare our own impressions."

GEORGE ELIOT

The Act of Being Present

Being present is a basic element of how we are together. We don't approach each other with preconceptions or projections, which is made easy by our total acceptance of each other. Being directly filled with the experience of something, rather than having expectations, leads to everything being fresh and often surprising. This is something that has always come naturally to us, perhaps because we focus on what is, rather than what has been or what might be. Doing so cuts out lots of drama, a style that has never appealed to either of us.

We don't take each other for granted, but rather seem to revel each time in the experience of the other. There is a mysterious aspect to this: each time feels new and even better than before. In our presence, everything is original and full of discovery.

Maude: The Wonderful Experience of Presence

When one is not filled with projections of how things should or could be, not filled with thoughts of the past or the future, then one winds up occupying the present. This act of being present in relationship brings many marvels with it. It leads to new and exciting experiences. It imbues shared experiences with a quality of creativity and co-creativity. When you combine these things, you achieve a marvelous sense of freedom of self and freedom of expression. When you can be gently present without defenses or any need to keep or raise barriers, it has an amazing and exhilarating effect.

We have this and yet it confounds both of us. We wonder how this can be, and at the same time it feels so easy and so natural. The ability to relax and be fully present seems to follow from the sense of undefended relating. We are in peace and trust and honesty because we are not assailed and we are not attacked. There is no pressure to be different than we are in our essence. So we are open and at peace in action and being.

I love this experience of being with you. I feel so supported in my own personal journey and so in union with you.

Phil: Presence

One of the remarkable things about you is how much I am drawn to being present when I am with you. I attribute that to your total acceptance: you offer a place for me to be myself — more than that, you encourage and rejoice in it. This is so rare a quality in this world that I joyfully respond to it.

I am present when I respond and react to what is actually happening, rather than using what the past has taught me, or reacting in order to bring about some future outcome. I don't claim to be anywhere near perfection in this; presence is a matter of the degree to which we are focused on the events in front of us. Neither do I claim that being present is always the most desirable state. Sometimes the future needs attention, too, so we try to control the world in order to make our imagined future come to pass. There are times when that is appropriate, but often it's like always ordering the next meal while you're eating the current one.

Being present is an important part of non-interference. By being present, the world just is, so I can let you be who you are, which in turn gives you the opportunity to be present. It's a virtuous circle, and having experienced it, why would either of us ever want it to be any other way? That is why I was so sure early on, even though I could not articulate the reason, that not only hadn't we argued, but that we probably never would.

There is another aspect of being present that we have both remarked on, which is the experience of newness that it brings. Nothing is ever the same, and it is very mysterious and counter-intuitive. You would think that settling in for a movie or walking around the park would become drab through familiarity. They don't. I surmise that they are intrinsically different – there is no Groundhog Day.

Another way to put this is that we are not constrained by our past, which gives us an extraordinary sense of potential, change and growth. By being open to what is present, we are open to change. It is not suppressed in favor of what has been, nor rejected in fear of what might happen. The result is a sense that we always have more to do and more to explore.

Maude: Come from Joy, Not Only from Loss

I've been wanting to write about our recent conversations of being in the present and how one gets there. You and I seem to come to the present through joy. We feel so free and natural with each other, that we come with ease fully into the present.

Often people are brought to an appreciation of the present moments through loss; something shocking happens, someone gets terribly ill suddenly, or we experience sudden and unexpected loss. This makes one appreciate the little things, to be aware of what is actually around, to be in the present.

One can achieve just such a sharp focus experience of reality through joy and celebration. We do.

I believe it could change the world if people would find ways to live with awareness, appreciation and gratefulness of that which is, from moment to moment. I do not need to lose you, or us, or our life, to love and appreciate the moments we get to share. Let us find our way to celebrate through joy!

Phil: The Path to the Present

We honor the present, or to rephrase it, we accept what is present; in other words, our direct experience in the moment. The present moment doesn't contain events that happened in the past. That cuts out a whole lot right there. And by not trying to direct the other, we relinquish attempts to manipulate the future. By refusing to be captured by regrets and yearnings from the past, and by accepting what is, rather than what might be, we allow ourselves to see and experience the other completely.

Here's the amazing part: by doing so, a freshness and vitality enters that I have never known before. Every day with you is a new and different experience. It is like taking a walk; it may be the same route, but I would never mistake Tuesday's walk for the one I took on Monday. And so with you: talking, sex, touching; all of these spring anew each time.

Maude: Each Day is So New with You!

Yes, I feel bright and shiny and new each time we are

together. It is rather amazing after this amount of time, but it does seems so fresh and such an adventure always. Neither of us take anything for granted. We haven't fallen asleep to some greater or lesser degree with each other. Our time together is always very exciting, while also being nourishing and soothing.

This must be another face of living in the present. I can't find any other explanation for it. Everything is so new because it is being created and co-created as we go. Feeling your presence is an amazing thing. It uplifts me. It re-assures me. It fascinates me. It surprises me. I never take it for granted, but I do know that you are always there with your whole self. There is no withdrawing, no abandoning. As you have said, we remain connected, both when we are physically together and when we are not. There is such peace in the experience of the present, unencumbered with things created solely by the mind or the past. How did we come to dwell in this place together? I can see that as one has these experiences, they are so attractive that one is pulled to remain there, to stay with something so good. But how did it come to be in our beginning?

Phil: The Present

We talk about presence and the present a lot, but it's a hard subject to pin down. I see it as an alternate, more basic way to view the world. As living beings, we have learned not only to react to the environment, but to remember the events so that we can react appropriately, and to predict events also. In other words, our model of the world contains a past and a future. Furthermore, we have invented language, wherein words are a stand-in for one or a bundle of experiences, and can also incorporate other words, leading to a very efficient way of storing information.

All this has been such a successful strategy that our attention routinely roams around the brain areas that manage the past and the future, interspersed with checking on linguistic summaries of the present. As a result, to experience the world in anything but verbal terms is very hard, but I want to point out some of its attributes.

My direct experience is unspeakable, by definition. It cannot be captured in words. It is like a reflection in a pool; if you reach out to grasp it, the ripples of words only hide the reflection. It is a hard discipline to leave it be.

It is primary. Our entire verbal and intellectual edifice is derived from this. It cannot be dismissed as of no consequence just because it has no place in our mental model of the world.

It has a timeless quality. The sense of time does not vanish completely (though it can be severely distorted by the flood of sensations), but our view of time is a construct of the mind, and it is as if I simultaneously experience two facets of reality: the flux of change (for time is change, nothing more or less) and an eternal, unchanging element. It's not eternal in the sense of lasting forever, but in the sense of being outside of time.

It's constantly new. This moment has never been before.

All that is preamble to talking about how we are together. We both choose to focus our attention on the present, whether it be the scenery while driving or the press of flesh on flesh, and we react in concert to an uncanny degree, far more than if it were viewed in the light of our past or our expectations. It is as if we are drinking from the same fountain, tasting the same wine.

To phrase it differently, our relationship consists of what is happening, not what did happen or what might happen. So many complications and misunderstandings are avoided by this. I thank you again and again.

Maude: Creating Something New

We've talked on a number of occasions about how being mutually present translates to co-creating. When we are both present together, union and presence, then something new comes into existence that never was before. And it happens each and every time. That is why we feel our experiences together are always better, although at the same time they feel as though they are as good as it possibly can get!

Phil: Being Open to the Present

Dear Maude,

We both awoke this morning from an especially restful sleep, and gave thanks to each other for the joy of each others' company, then had the following conversation, which I want to capture before it escapes me.

Me: *How come this happens?*

You: *Because we're open to the present.*

Me: *So we are not yearning for how it formerly was, or wishing for some future state. But if that is the correct approach, suppose you're with an unsuitable partner – complaining, abusive, whatever – doesn't accepting the present remove all motivation to change? Isn't the future ideal a great motivator?*

You: *By being fully present, you see the behavior for what it is, and have the choice to change the situation.*

Maude: Peace and Love are Strong Deep Feelings

We were standing together this morning hugging before separating, and it was such a deep and warm sharing. I started thinking that if people knew what strong experiences peace and love are, perhaps they wouldn't be so attracted to conflict, anxiety, drama and tension. I think often people equate strong feelings with the negativity they create. Maybe in order to have the sense of having feelings, or caring deeply, people create problems and conflicts to reassure themselves that they care or are cared for. I know it sounds turned around, but I think this is often the case. If we can communicate how strong our shared experiences are, maybe it could click in some people's minds and they would move toward exchanges that are filled with love and generate peace. Maybe they could 'get it' that what they are seeking doesn't come from generating drama or illusory problems. But rather, that it comes from being present and actually experiencing what is really there, who the other truly is as a person. It's great to experience the joy of sharing who you are and being appreciated for that; of not being pushed or pulled, changed or manipulated, but just having someone rejoice in your person and to share with you theirs. Maybe we can find the words to illuminate for others this miraculous experience that we share!

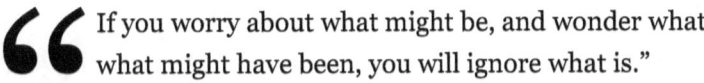 If you worry about what might be, and wonder what what might have been, you will ignore what is."

AUTHOR UNKNOWN

Acceptance

Acceptance is an essential aspect of why we work so well together. By accepting the other just as they are, as someone different and uniquely separate from ourselves, we have found a path of freedom and peace. We simply accept each other's being and actions completely. To do so is an act of trust in the other, a belief in their positive intentions. We seem to have bypassed all the attempts at shaping and molding the other that so frequently characterize relationships. We don't try to remake the other in our own image. For us, then, acceptance is not an action, it is refraining from interference and control. By doing so, this leaves the other person free to be and express their true self — a very liberating experience.

Phil: Non-interference

For me, it starts with non-interference — the position of allowing you to act as you choose, without my attempting to influence your decisions, big or small, as you travel through life.

I do this because I do not want to control you. Why would I take on the burden of that responsibility?

I do this because you are not a child who must be taught the ways of the world for your own good.

I do this because of the pleasure of experiencing your views, pleasures and desires. Why would I want to narrow my world by making those more like my own?

I do this because I do not feel threatened by you, physically, financially, emotionally. I started with an assumption of trust, and the more time passes the more I am confirmed in this. Another way to put this is that you are practicing the same non-interference.

How cool that you do this too! I am not assailed by criticisms or put-downs; I feel accepted, seen, honored. Because of this, I am able to express myself, be myself, live my life without feeling in any way diminished. On the contrary, I am enhanced by the communication between us that flows so effortlessly because your complete acceptance means there is nothing to inhibit its passage.

Maude: Calm and Peace

Dear Phil,

Our time together is so filled with a sense of calm and

peace. We don't seem to spend any time on power struggles or on one of us trying to be "right". I never feel I have to defend myself against anything coming from you and can therefore be free to fully share myself. In fact, I feel both honored and appreciated for who I am. As time goes on, and we continue to have more and more of the experience of struggle-free relating, we build a trust that this is how it is and will remain for us. What a miracle, and it seems so easy. We just let go and let be.

Phil: Demands

My Dear Maude,

I make what to many might be an outrageous claim: *make no demands upon the other. That's none, nil, nada, zilch.*

I've spent years with the bathroom half-renovated? You keep checking email when coffee is ready? He leaves his clothes lying around? Who are you to control his habits? She takes 20 minutes to put on make-up? That's just what she needs to feel comfortable.

With you, the experience of being able to act without engendering your approval or disapproval leads to an extraordinary freedom that I have never experienced before in a relationship: the possibility of being myself. Furthermore, it is cumulative; the longer we are together, the more assured we are of this, and the more we are each able to express ourselves.

Maude: I Rejoice in Who You Are

You mentioned making no demands. That is a description of not doing something. I don't have the feeling generally of avoiding doing something. There is an experience that for you is described by making no demands. I look there and I see me sitting comfortably inside my center. I take pleasure in you sitting right in your center. I don't wish to make you me. I rejoice in who and what you are, which is not me. I don't want to change you or your actions.

Phil: Agreement

Dear Maude,

There's nothing to report – we just continue to get on magnificently.

WAIT! That's the weird thing – how does this happen?

I want to distinguish between disagreements and arguments. The former is possible, the latter unimaginable. Why would I want to persuade you to do something against your will? When I accept that what you say is how it is for you, I fully accept your reported reality and do not discount it as less important than mine. This requires two things: that I accept you as fully equal to me, not in skills and desires but in rights and consciousness, and that I trust you to be truthful.

Maude: Conversation with Carole

My Dear Phil,

At the same time we were having our talks this weekend, I was sharing with Carole about things happening in her relationship.

She had come to the same conclusion we had. The specifics of a particular situation are not what is important. Rather it is the meaning and value that are of consequence.

We also talked about the issue of lists and list making. It seems we all have our lists, things we note about another person, things we've been right about, where unfairness or injustice have taken place, or where we haven't been acknowledged or ... all the big and small transgressions.

We may not even be aware that we have these lists. However, in the moment when we are faced with something negative about ourselves, criticism or someone else's list, our list comes popping up full of things and ready to go!

The moral? Lists never do anything but bring forth other lists. List making is to be avoided. Let the lists and the specifics go. Look for harmony, truth, beauty and goodness. We can develop our attraction to that which is Real, of meaning and value. The rest are merely creations of the mind. If we are not attracted to discord and disharmony, we won't give life to those parts within us. It can be as easy as developing your appetite, your attraction.

Phil: Criticism

Dear Maude,

You talk about using lists as a defense against criticism.

I read recently how damaging criticism is — that we need five compliments to offset a single criticism. But any criticism is an attempt to change the other person, to say that they are not perfect, that you don't accept certain shapes or sounds or behaviors. The other person may compromise, attack in return, withdraw, or brush it off, but whatever the response, the action is pernicious; it makes one guarded, it eats at the soul. Every criticism of another is a denial of who they are, and a non-acceptance of the same. I've broken up with a number of people feeling that I had lost myself; I no longer knew who I was or what I wanted.

This has an effect on the critic, too. They are yearning after something, they cannot live in the world as it is, they cannot accept their partner as is, they want more, better, different. In short, they are captured by the past, and cannot be present.

I know you much prefer positive conversations, so let me talk about the opposite. With you, there is nothing like that. I feel so at liberty to be myself, and this co-exists with a companionship that is so free and easy. There is a peculiar paradox here: by being still, by not struggling for what we think we want, we get closer and closer. It is as if we are naturally drawn to one another, yet any action causes a movement away from the center. The more still we are, the more we partake in a harmonious flow through life.

Maude: I Woke from My Dream and was Annoyed

Dear Phil,

I woke up this morning from a dream in which I was low level irritated, really annoyed with someone. It was that attitude of diffuse impatience with a person that is so very common in the world. I think a lot of people spend a lot of time feeling that way toward their partners and the people they live with or work with. I woke to that sensation and to you sleeping next to me. I realized that I never, and I do truly mean never feel that way with you.

This may sound silly, but I think that is wonderful, absolutely amazing! I never feel impatience or irritation with you. Our time together is always full of joy, full of goodness. I am happy and peaceful and comfortable whenever we are together. That can be at the end of a work day, over a weekend of being together or two weeks of traveling and being together all the time.

We are never short or harsh with each other. It seems we are never irritated or annoyed. What is this different way of being together that seems so natural, so right? We could spread so much peace and goodness if we could pass on to others how to relate in this manner.

Phil: The Golden Rule

I wonder what the prerequisites are for this level of agreement. On reflection, I think it needs a full belief in the golden rule, "Treat others as you wish to be treated", which describes an equivalence between me and you, that we are both equally important.

To act based on this, you have to put yourself in their place for a moment. A more succinct term for this is empathy, a skill that develops over the years (though it may stall or fall back in some). Furthermore, it seems likely to me that to increase in empathy is to approach nearer to God, spirit, union or whatever term works for you.

Maude: And There's Talking to Each Other

We talk with each other all the time about everything.

We have always talked and shared our thoughts and our feelings. This has been for us a very natural and easy way to be together. I think this flow of communication that we share so lightly is actually a very important component in our union.

Your interest in communicating and in knowing and understanding me and our experiences together, has always deeply attracted me to you. Your ability to listen, as well as to express your thoughts and feelings, endears you to my heart.

Being with you is such a sweet pleasure!

Phil: The Freedom to Say Anything

I love what you say about talking because I have had the "we need to talk" speech from so many other people.

So what's the difference? Was I mutated by a bombard-ment of cosmic rays? No, I think everyone has, somewhere at least, a need to talk, to express themselves, to be seen. To never do so would be a life of existential loneliness. People may hold back out of shame, embarrassment or guilt, but we all need that contact at least on occasion to feel connected to others.

One reason the talking is so easy and fluid with us is the complete acceptance that we've talked about many times before. There are no mine-fields, no dangerous areas, no taboo subjects, no demands to talk or be silent or respond or be a particular way, and this is such a liberating thing. It's this way for both of us, and leads to great freedom and joy.

 Happiness can exist only in acceptance."

GEORGE ORWELL

Effortlessness

We frequently hear about the importance of working on a relationship, but so often that is taken to mean effort, struggle and conflict. That is not our experience. Why would we want to go there? When we have different desires or opinions or goals, we each present our case, offering our reasons and emotions, and hear the other's position too. By experiencing each other's ideas, our reality changes, and through this process we come to a mutual viewpoint.

There is no conflict here in the sense of defending a position or resisting any new idea, and so there is no sense of struggle; in fact, the feeling is quite the opposite. There is a feeling of pleasure at engaging with the other and a sense of an emerging solution. The end result feels like a creation that is neither of ours, but is instead something that is grander than either of us could have dreamt.

This happens in every aspect of our lives, from deciding how to spend the day to the largest challenges of life. In all these choices, we actively pick peace, trust and union over effort and struggle.

Maude: What Makes Us So Special?

Dear Phil,

We are gentle and loving and kind with each other. We do this without effort and with very little consciousness of behaving in this manner. We do not seem to be irritated or annoyed with each other. This may also come from accepting each other entirely as we are, and not wishing that the other would somehow be different or act differently.

It is a mystery. It does take two to make something like this happen. I believe that we have both equally allowed this to occur. And yet, it was not with hard work, as so many people suggest is necessary to develop and maintain a relationship.

In fact, there is no sense of effort at all. It is a mystery!

Phil: Don't Work on your Relationship!

My Dear Maude,

Your delightful list of reasons why we are special ends with its effortless nature, that it doesn't take work. So many people write about the necessity of working on a relationship; I reject that idea. Working on something is what I call a job, not a relationship.

We never feel the need to work things out in the sense of resolving a conflict. Firstly, we are in agreement on things large and small to an uncanny degree, but when we're not, they are never seen as a conflict; we simply talk about it, and out of that, comes a conclusion. It happens every time.

But how we do this is hard to pin down. Maybe it's like riding a bicycle. At first, you fall over all the time; later, staying balanced becomes second nature. We prefer the peace of co-existence; the drama of alienation has no attraction for us. How and why we do this is unclear to me; did we learn this, or is it in our natures? Certainly, to do this requires a degree of non-attachment, and also an understanding of how much influence one can and can't have with another person.

We both revel in the pleasure of the other, and feel no need to change them; indeed, their difference is a source of pleasure and wonder. This non-interference is a key aspect of this lack of conflict.

Maude: There are Paradoxes

There are paradoxes associated with how we are with each other. We do not experience our relationship as something that takes work or that we have to consciously apply techniques to achieve. And yet it is something that we have to actively do. It is something that we have gotten better at. Our togetherness seems more mature and deeper. At the same time that seems impossible, as each experience is the best anything could ever be. The way we are is joyous and smooth. It is so very full of peace and comfort on an abiding spirit level.

Maude: Allowing it to Happen

This morning we were embracing before going into the day and it was so dear and sweet.

You said "How did we get so lucky?"

The first thing that came into my head was that in order for something to happen, you have to allow it. This goes in the same direction as that which allows us to experience such a peaceful and non conflictual together-ness. We don't come with expectations of specifics; we don't insist on or demand certain activities or words or actions. We flow through the together time actually experiencing what happens. This is always bigger and better than anything either one of us could have come up with in advance.

In the same way, I think people often walk right past

opportunities and potential partners because they have images and preconceptions of what they want and need, that leave out the possibility for something unexpected and unpredictable to happen.

We did really get blessed to find each other, but we also let it happen. We went with it as it grew and took on form. We allowed creativity and presence to rule.

And so here we are!

Phil: Letting Things Happen

My Dear Maude,

I think we are on to something important in this discussion of allowing something to happen. By insisting on a particular movie or director or genre rather than a preference, certain possibilities are ruled out, but by being open to alternatives, anything is possible. This is a subtle point. It's different from suppressing one's desires, different from taking a position of not caring, and different from freezing into inaction. It's about being open to other possibilities, of not being locked into a mindset of how things have to be.

We had a discussion about us this morning that picked up this idea.

We just seem to get better and better together; again and again we have a never-before experience of union, and yet next time we discover something fresh and new. This feels very mysterious, and contrary to the way things work in the world. You pointed out that we act similarly to how we behave outside; we don't have rules about what must be or expectations about what should or will happen, and this allows a spontaneous flow into states that we cannot imagine beforehand.

Maude: Spontaneity and No Rules

Dear Phil,

We often bring each other greeting cards, always looking for new ways to express our feelings to each other. Last night I gave you two cards. It felt like a two card night.

You remarked that this was a perfect example of the spontaneity that abides between us. You thought it was connected to there being 'no rules'. You said, "we have no rules, no rules that say one card a night, or no cards, or you should do this or that..."

I have to agree that we indeed play it all in the moment, just following our feelings, with no particular program. Neither of us seems to need to put preconceptions upon the other or within our relationship. We always have a new co-creative experience when we are together.

And yet, for this wonderful experience of creating together, we do nothing in particular. It just seems to happen so simply, so naturally.

If you don't fill up the space with plans and concepts and ideas and expectations, then the moment itself is pregnant with creativity, full of pulsing newness, of life.

Our life, our time together, is a miracle, each and every moment it occurs!

❝ When you struggle with your partner, you are struggling with yourself. Every fault you see in them touches a denied weakness in yourself."

DEEPAK CHOPRA

Union

There are times when we experience the world not just from our own viewpoint, but also as another, one that is not me and not you, but rather a merging of the two of us. There is a sense of simultaneous consciousness of me and of us.

How does this come about? We honor each other as

separate people, and at the same time open ourselves fully to one another. We find that when we are not defended and can flourish as ourselves in the presence of the other, something new can come into being — a place of joy, harmony and union. This seems almost magical because it appears to be outside the basic laws of physics. We are still two, each of us ourselves as always, and yet we have also become one. We experience the separate and the unified at the same time.

Maude: Balance

The other day I was feeling such deep union with you and the word "balance" came into my mind. It seems to me that neither of us is more present, or taking up more space in the union, or having stronger desires for something specific, or pushing for some direction.

We seem to be so equally there, so completely balanced in our beingness with the other, that a third presence emerges. This third presence is our union. It covers an area that is not the separate personality of me or of you, both of which are fully present, but rather of another. This third presence is one where the lines between you and me blur and melt together. This is experienced not just on the mindal or spirit level, but even on the physical.

This balance, where neither push nor pull are present, seems to be a key to the experience we share. And yet where does it come from? We seem to do it so naturally.

I think an important component is the utter respect and appreciation for the other as an individual.

Maude: Long Sessions of Talking in Union

We have these wonderful long sessions of talking. We achieve such a closeness that it feels above the regular level of human contact. We seem to enter another realm where time is altered. It is much the same as states of being we achieve when we are sexual.

These long talking experiences create a deep feeling of connectedness. We find ever deepening pathways of discussion and seem to be able to flow from one to the other without boundaries or separation.

The time factor is almost startling. We can feel like long periods of time have gone by and find that on the clock it has been very short. Or we can float in this ecstatic exchange with no feeling of time passing at all.

These experiences are blissful and filled with a sense of peace and well being. The sense of being merged with another is so basic. It feels like we are experiencing something that is very real, that could be there in life on an ongoing basis.

How do we find the way to share about this and bring it more into existence? It is the question that comes up right after an Enlightenment Intensive. How do we bring it into everyday life?

We seem to have found a way to live on a daily basis with this between us as a very real experience, one of no conflict and much joy.

How do we spread this in our lives and to others?

Phil: The Puzzle of Union

Dear Maude,

Yes, the time phenomenon is very strange, but I'll put it down to being intensely present.

More puzzling to me is the sense of union, of experiencing another being that is not me and not you; at the same time, I am also aware of myself. This has happened to me just a few times in my past, but with you, it's a regular occurrence. It's puzzling because I have no place in my scientific cosmology for it; my brain says maybe it's the experience of chemicals designed to promote pair bonding such as oxytocin or vasopressin. Maybe it's a hallucination, a desirable illusion designed to promote sex and reproduction. It's just a subjective phenomenon, a trick of the light.

Against this, there is the claim of many mystics that we are all one. "I am he as you are he as you are me and we are all together."

And lastly, I say no, this is my primary experience. There is only experience in my world; all those theories are ways to explain and classify it, nothing more, so ignoring my experience in favor of the theories is a dangerous route. Here, I also have to refer to the Enlightenment Intensives, the epitome of chopping through words to reach the direct experience.

So I have this dialogue in my head and this experience in my body, and sometimes it makes me feel like an Escher illusion.

Maude: Ah Yes, the Experience of Union!

Dear One,

I agree. The validity and authority of experience is at the core of recognizing that which is.

It is really quite extraordinary to have the experience of union with you over and over and over. This beingness that comes through you and me is radiant and true. It vibrates with Reality. You are so honest and good. I can open my heart and my mind to the present with you, with full assurance of honor, truth, safety, joy, and unending adventure.

Just being with you every night and every morning, and all night long, is such exquisite happiness, such peace. When we come together, we beam light. We are adding to the overall goodness by living this union.

It is joy living in presence with you.

Maude: There is Not the Slightest Question About It

When we talk about finding a language, of developing the words to speak of our experience, neither of us has any doubt of what we mean, that we experience the same thing. We search for ways to communicate about it. We talk about it and write about it. We know that we have the same experience. There's not the slightest doubt about it.

Actually, that is in and of itself rather remarkable. How can something so elusive be so definite for us, so clear?

And yet it is, unshakably, most certainly clear. We both experience the same thing without giving up anything from our separate individualities.

This union is so solid, so strong, so fully present. It is unmistakable.

This union is so soft, so gentle, so firm.

So mutual.

Phil: Our Common Experience

Dear Maude,

I want to expand on your post about joint experience.

I find this issue of complete agreement to be very strange. When I talk, you always concur with my descriptions, and furthermore, this is not at all surprising; in fact, the surprise would be if there were any significant differences. This is true the other way, too; you describe how it was for you, and I go "Uh-huh, uh-huh" in concurrence. Now you and I have led different lives, have different bodies with sex organs of different types, and whose nervous systems are not connected. So either there's a lot of coincidence going on, or WE'RE HAVING THE SAME EXPERIENCE.

For events like watching a movie or going to a play, we also "experience the same thing", but in those cases, we often differ in interpretation or meaning; our experience of the event has been mediated by our history and viewpoint. But this is something different; when we come together, it is as if you and I actually touch, and I don't just mean physically, but in some other dimensions as well, so there is a surface of contact, and our descriptions of it must necessarily correspond. (One shape would be the inverse of the other, but that's a simple mapping.)

Maybe I'm getting too abstract, mathematical, scientific and theoretical here, but that's my language, I guess, and as you say, we are engaged in finding a language for this experience. However, don't take my language for the event; it is but a pale attempt to grasp at our reality.

Maude: From Zero to Take Off in No Time at All

We seem to be able to go from the lightest touch to full-blown union in a matter of time that is so infinitesimal, it is not really measured by sequence at all.

I was noticing last night as we began to make love, that we barely touched and then we transported (in an almost 'beam me up Scottie' way) to outer space. The night before, I felt like I opened some non-physical eyes and looked around. I saw stars or pinpoints of light, and we seemed to be out there among them, somewhere near the outer regions. This "we" I just referred to is another being that is connected physically, mentally and in spirit. Time is different, and so is space. It is not that there is no sense of time. It is more like time is accelerated to 3 or 4 times its normal experience. I can feel certain points on my body distinctly. At the same time, I feel that most of us has melted together in some way. I can think thoughts in my own individual mind, but there is a place where we are together in the mind circuitry. The mutual spirit song is something I haven't yet explored, except that I sense it is there to be explored.

This all feels so wonderful and mysterious, but also very real. It is a bonding and strengthening event. I believe it rides underneath everything else we do and feel.

Phil: The Reality of Union

My Dear Maude,

This experience of union is a mysterious joy. I have fleetingly known it before, but with you, it is a regular occurrence. Yet the rational scientist in me asks if it is an illusion, a trick that nature has dreamed up to facilitate sex, bonding, family and cooperation. Our senses can often fool us; why is this not the case here as well?

Let me offer some reasons.

"The fact precedes the explanation" is a phrase I coined in my twenties to mean that the raw experience of the world trumps any theory. At some point I have to take a stand and say that my experience of union is real. It is stronger when we are in physical contact, and strongest when sexual. It is as though the point of contact between you and me *is* us. I want to be very clear here: this is not the same as feeling your body; that happens at the same time, but is not the same as the joint experience. There is a strong feeling of mutuality, that what is taking place arises not from you or me; we are but observers of the event.

You and I are complex systems. When two complex

systems are joined, interactions and possibilities are created that do not exist in the individual cases. Two eyes offer depth perception beyond that of one eye. A finger and thumb can perform manipulations that one digit cannot.

The idea of a supra-individual consciousness is not prevalent in Western culture, though it has been written about in many places.

This is a rather intellectual response, I know, but it is a radical change in world-view that we're talking about here, and I feel the need to provide a sound basis for it, both for my own benefit and for use with other people.

Maude: I Wanted to Thank You

We had such a transcendent experience last night while making love and I wanted to thank you. We reach a place, not in thought, but in actual experience that impinges upon the Divine. It is the experience of the infinite. There is a quality of never endingness and there is no recognizable sequence. Hence there is no experience of time as we usually know it. We experience that there is no end in that 'place' where we go in union. There is no end except the physical material limitations we have by the nature of what we are.

I want to thank you for allowing me to go there. It is an experience that you need a partner to achieve. There are other ways to have this experience, but the path that we are walking calls for a partner. I have always believed that this type of direct experience of Reality was possible between people, but I have never before had a partner who wanted to walk that path together. It is such ecstasy. It opens up the vistas of all that is beyond.

And again, thank you!

Phil: Union

I want to write about union. It's a difficult subject, especially for me, because it flies in the face of everyday experience, but time after time we have this experience of union, of oneness. I want to be clear on one point: there is no loss of self; instead, the experience is of myself and of us simultaneously. I don't mean a sense of you and your body. It's a sense of a third autonomous center that only comes into existence (or is perceived, don't know which) when my own ego and intentionality are quieted. As I have written before, we are in complete agreement on this experience.

So what is going on here? Two factors come into play for me. Firstly, I want to point out that experience trumps theory, or as I put it in my youth, "the fact precedes the explanation". Any theory has to accommodate the facts; if it doesn't, it is deficient. Of course, illusions may exist — the car wheels caught on film appear to be spinning backwards — but the entire body of theory exists IN ORDER TO explain our experiences, so they must have a certain validity. Secondly, I like theories that explain the facts of my world; they organize it, make sense of it, and have useful predictive powers.

Bearing these two in mind, I propose that both realities

are true: that we are both separate and one. This contradicts Aristotelian logic. Tough. Light is both a wave and a particle, which doesn't make sense, either, but the evidence for it is overwhelming.

In order to make this more palatable, let me offer a metaphor: we are like pages in a book. Every page appears unique; it has its own number, its own words, its own meaning, yet we more easily see the book as the unit. Is there a similar one-ness to the world that we are failing to see?

Just as we can come up with a list of differences between you and me, so we can come up with a list of equivalences: culture, nationality, race, DNA, and the very atoms of which we are composed. So maybe we are both an individual and a species; an individual and a life-form; an individual and a collection of atoms. Our culture emphasizes individuality, especially in America, so our upbringing teaches us to only see that fact.

But what constitutes an individual becomes less clear-cut the more it is examined. For instance, a single person is not just an arrangement of 10 trillion human cells, but also contains ten times as many microbial cells that are essential to well-being. Some researchers think of our bodies as super-organisms, rather than one organism teeming with hordes of subordinate invertebrates.

In the West, our belief system is built on an egocentric framework. To admit the experience of union it is necessary to expand that framework to allow for its possibility, otherwise any experience of union will be overlooked or dismissed. Having made room for it, we also need a non-egoistic situation where it can emerge. Sex is one such, but it can be found in intimate conversations or communing with nature.

In the West, we use words for explanations and answers, but they fail to satisfy in answering the Big Questions because language works best as a divisive tool. Words classify the world into this and not this, which makes them very unsuited to describe union, or one-ness. Additionally, a word is not the thing; we can only use a word like a pointer, so expecting words to guide us to union is optimistic. Instead, the opposite is true: silence, listening, observing, being open to the present, can guide us there. The knowledge of one-ness is experiential, not verbal.

Maude: Union and Peace

This wonderful experience of union that we are partaking of seems to find its verification for both of us in the experience of Reality. There is no necessary or possible validation for something of this nature, other than direct experience. It is so full. Such an encounter with truth, beauty and goodness leaves no questions of veracity. It is to be treasured, explored and most definitely shared.

I feel stronger, better and more able to love others, as a result of this union of ours. Perhaps these words are too sweeping and sound like I have become lost in this shared merging. Regardless, I know that I am clear and grounded in my everyday world and that I feel like a carrier of peace. I seem to be filled beyond filling with feelings of calm, joy and love. And most of all, I experience an abiding peace. I feel like this peace is something that is part of that which is real, but also that we have co-created it, brought it into the world of time and space, if you will.

I find it astonishing that something of this meta-physical nature can be so fully here in the physical, material world. In fact, it seems to flow into existence often, as we wrap around each other; as we come in close, closer physical contact. It causes a fascination within me to experience directly just how united mind, matter and spirit can be.

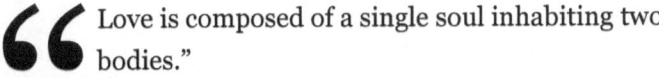 Love is composed of a single soul inhabiting two bodies."

ARISTOTLE

Peace

It may seem a bit strange to be talking about peace in the context of relationships. Nevertheless, the actual experience of peace has been life-altering for us, and it has come to us through the way we are together. We both arrived here through different routes: Phil through struggle, and Maude through family example, but no matter what the starting point, everyone can come to it.

There is much said about peace, and yet we can't help but wonder how often people have actually experienced it in their lives. Once you have this experience, it is so powerful, so all-encompassing, so wonderful, you would never want to dwell anywhere else. Once tasted, peace is so alluring that it naturally crowds out all attraction towards dissonance and disharmony. And when you can take the hand of another and walk that path together, you see that the whole world could be changed by just that act.

Maude: The Attraction of Peace

If I were to describe how we are together, the primary thing would be peace. Indeed, we have found a way to coexist in a place of balance and harmony that both supports and encourages each of us in our own personal development. We are not contributing to discord and dissonance. I do not find that I am ever pushed to respond from my lowest of reactions, from the animal parts of me that are lurking below the surface. Instead, I feel that I am living in my best part, in my higher realms of personality actualization. Your very presence and the experience of the kind of relating that we do so easily and naturally has landed me in a world colored by meaning and value. We have the experience of relationship filled with peace, harmony, joy, love, truth, beauty and goodness. We are manifesting our core values, that which feels real to me. We do this without any energy going toward the illusory, the imagined energies of anger, conflict, fear. And yet, there is no struggle involved. As actively as we live this together, it feels as though it is the easiest thing possible. And the most attractive.

The attraction toward harmony and lack of tensions is a critical component in being together as we are. It has to pull you toward it. You have to want to leave the juice of conflict behind you. You have to find a way to allow peace to occur.

Phil: Peace is Being not Doing

I think peace is more a case of being than doing. In the world, I struggle with the seized-up bolt, go to work, balance the checkbook and deal with the termites in the eaves, but being peaceful is a state that you and I are in, not an activity. It seems that we're just plain lucky to have this peace between us – graced, to use a more delicate term. Yet it also feels intentional, that we do something to create this harmony. I think that when we are together, you and I open up to each other, and in turn fully accept all that is offered. This makes a space where it is possible to be undefended, and creates that deep peaceful feeling, not just sometimes, but every time we are together. This is so wonderful, because instead of needing to put effort into the relationship, I am revived, and can apply all my energy to the challenges of the world.

Maude: Peace Brings Joy

The energies that we are filled with while spending time with one another are both sustaining and nourishing. When people can relate without struggle, without the desire for power or to overpower, a buoying force pervades the exchange. This visceral experience of calm, love and peace transcends fear and anxiety. It supports a trust of being present with your whole person. It supports undefended participation in everything. It brings joy.

When people can relate in this way with each other, new unique creations occur.

Phil: Where Do Arguments Come From?

My Dear Maude,

I contrast how we are with people who act like Dr. Jekyll and Mr. Hyde. We have both had partners like this. One moment, everything is fine, then POW! Something sets them off, and someone unrecognized appears: maybe hysterical, maybe furious, maybe withdrawn.

There are several ways we react to this. One is to defend against the attack, to fight back, to deny the accusations. A second is to feel guilty, to feel the attack is justified in some way. Maybe I should have called her back? Maybe I shouldn't have said that? It's easy to react this way because sometimes we do screw up, and in such cases, this is the only way out. A third way is to try and fix it, to do whatever it takes, because she is your partner and she is in pain, and because you want normal service to resume as soon as possible.

It was with A., a very volatile partner, that I first noticed the rock. When she got angry, I wouldn't let myself get dragged in. I would not let myself be affected by it. Oh, there were times it went on so long that I reacted in anger at the whole mess, but in general, I could just let it wash over me, could wait it out, be a rock in the stream.

I write about all this because we don't do it. Ever. In its place is a constancy, one that we both remarked on after getting to know each other. I love the consistency. Of course there is variability: sometimes you are tired or ill or quiet, but I never feel that you have changed in how you are and how you see me, and this is profoundly calming and peaceful. Thank you.

Maude: Talking and Developing a Taste for Peace

Dear Phil,

I love how we talk about things and just seem to come to resolutions or decisions. This has always been a basic aspect of our time together and maybe this is one of the critical factors. We have always really talked with each other. We have a comfortable and natural style of talking over things with each other and forming a plan of action or coming to a decision. I think often when people are feeling upset with each other or angry or misunderstood, it is because they do not really stay in communication. They have to guess what the other is thinking or feeling and this leads to distance, fear and lack of harmony. If commun-icating becomes a natural part of how people are with each other, then many of the conflicts and problems will probably never even arise. Can something this simple really be an antidote to so many problems? Yes, I think it can.

Another thing is that neither of us is really attracted to conflict or fighting or any of those kinds of energies. We are strongly attracted to peace and union and harmony and kindness and happiness and love. We both seem to be totally fulfilled with these emotions and experiences and have no attraction at all to the chemical rushes associated with the other. I think very often, people have come to associate these negative feelings with having feelings at all. For this reason, they seek for the strong rushes of discord. Perhaps it wouldn't be all that difficult to work on switching attractions. To develop a taste for harmony!

Phil: The Banquet

My Dear Maude:

I love what you say about peace and how we are. I still cannot distinguish who brought what to the table, but I am so grateful for the banquet, and say thanks that we are graced with this feast. At the same time, it does seem that we are responsible for cooking this up together.

I feel that the recipe for peace is so simple that anyone can grasp it and taste it, and once they do, will choose to remain at the table. And as others join us in such a way, we will feed the entire world.

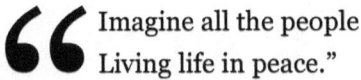 Imagine all the people
Living life in peace."

JOHN LENNON

Conclusion

Putting these ideas together was an exhilarating and informative experience for us. We hope you enjoyed what you read, and found words and ideas that resonated with and inspired you. These ideas have power, and if you allow them to work within you, they will lead to transformative experiences. They can be applied not just between partners, but between people everywhere. By being open, honest and accepting, you make room for others to live more harmoniously. As respect for each other increases, the world becomes a more peaceful place. This energy is more catching and more attractive than conflict and anger.

Peace is an experience with the power to spread through the world. We can see a day when this comes to pass. We hope you will join us in making this happen.

About the Authors

Phil and Maude Mayes live in Santa Barbara, California, having started in London, England and New York City respectively. Phil is a software engineer and photographer. Maude works with adults with developmental disabilities and owns a business importing and selling antique European linens and laces. They are a happily married couple who have both had previous marriages and several long-term relationships. The striking difference between their marriage and previous relationships caused much reflection and discussion between them, and was the genesis of this book.

Let's Talk

We hope you've enjoyed this book and will let all your friends know about it. We invite you to communicate with us about relationships and ways to bring peace to the world. Let's contribute to everyone's understanding of the power that harmonious living can bring!

Visit us at http://www.PhilandMaude.com